Make Money Installing LED Holiday Lighting
A Guide to Creating a Christmas Lights Installation Business

By Dennis Harvey and Brennan Morrow

CHAPTER OUTLINE

Introduction. Why Start a L.E.D. Holiday Light Business?

This chapter explains the growth of the holiday lighting industry, generally defines your market, and explores the growth of holiday lighting over the past ten years.

Chapter 1. Advantages of Using Energy Efficient Holiday Lighting

Reviews the history of incandescent lighting for holiday lighting. It then goes into detail about holiday lighting technology and reviews the differences between incandescent and LED lights.

Chapter 2. Starting your Business 101

This is written for the beginning business person. It discusses choosing naming the business, pros and cons of different legal entity types, setting up banking etc.

Chapter 3. Estimating your Startup Costs

A detailed estimate sheet for startup costs. Includes materials, legal costs, office equipment, advertising and marketing, and lighting materials.

Chapter 4. A Five Year Business Plan and Projection

A complete five year business plan projection to include, material cost, labor, gross sales and gross profit. A spreadsheet allows business owners to make their own projections over a five year period.

Chapter 5. Prospecting The Potential Market

Illustrates low-cost ways to determine what potential markets and how to reach them. Helps project potential gross sales and estimated net profits based on the amount and type of advertising used.

Chapter 6. Residential and Commercial Marketing

One of the keys to success in any industry is marketing. This chapter shows seven detailed marketing ideas that work together to motivate customers to use holiday lighting services.

Chapter 7. Working With Suppliers

A step by step guide on which suppliers to use. Websites, phone numbers and exact product numbers. Includes L.E.D. lights, timers, wreaths, garlands, cords and installation equipment.

Chapter 8. Hiring and Training Installers

Includes how to choose and assemble a workforce. How to train installers. Step-by-step specifics of installing L.E.D. lights, garlands, wreaths, trees and shrubs.

Chapter 9. Estimating Jobs

Provides information on measuring a job, interviewing the potential customer, estimating trees and shrubs and overall pricing of business services. How to write a bid and sales follow up are addressed.

9.1 Work Order example
9.2 Commercial estimate example

Chapter 10. How To Get Referrals and Repeat Business

This chapter includes managing mailing lists, value-added promotion and customer follow up.

Chapter 11. Putting It All Together: A Timeline for Success!

This is the wrap up of all the chapters, showing a chronological timeline for the maximum success of your business.

Starting Your L.E.D. Holiday Light Business
Why Start Your Own Holiday Light Business

The Holiday Lighting Industry has grown over 20% per year for the last 10 years. Although it is not accurately tracked, it is estimated that the industry does over a Billion Dollars a year. That's a lot of lights.

Many people who hire Holiday Lighting contractors to install Christmas Decorations could be described as upper middle class who simply want nice looking professionally installed holiday displays at their home or business. Many are dual income families that place a high value on their personal time. They feel their time is worth more than their money.

In addition, they don't mow their lawn, do their landscaping, clean their gutters or paint their houses. We are a service driven society.

There are many different types of lights and decorations that can be installed at a home or business. Most likely you are familiar with this kind of lighting. Incandescent lighting has been around since the late 1800s, and a technology that has changed very little since then.

In 2002 we started a business in Bend, Oregon installing a different type of Holiday Light. We used L.E.D. lights (light emitting diode). It is a microchip used for lighting computers, printers and cell phones. Have you ever had a L.E.D. light in your electronic equipment fail? They last longer than the equipment they support.

They were developed by an engineer on the East Coast who was tired of dealing with the frustration of the old lighting technology. The lights always failed. If one light went out they all went out. Then he had to go through 100 lights to find out the one that was bad. In addition they were made of glass and broke easily.

If you have installed Christmas Lighting, you probably have experienced the same frustration. L.E.D. Holiday Lights first came on the market in 2001 and were only sold commercially.

In the last 13 years retailers have added to their holiday displays and can be found in most Big Box retailers. Costco, Sam's Club, Lowe's, Home Depot and others. The last 3 years Costco in Bend sold out before Thanksgiving.

We used this technology to target market the Holiday Lighting Installation Business.

This book is designed to take you through the steps on how to Start Your Own Business, Or Expand Your Existing Business by providing additional services during the slow winter season.

This business is ideal as an ad-on service for Landscapers, Landscape Maintenance, Painters, Window Cleaners, Pest Control Operators, Fence Installers, Pool Service Providers to name a few. Almost all outside contracting business can add this additional service.

It is a great way for an existing business to add to your customer service base, and provide additional work for your employees during the slow winter season.

Providing this service is not difficult. once you learn the basics of <u>MARKETING AND INSTALLATION.</u> These are key steps that you will learn in this book.

Whether you are looking to start up a business, or add additional services to your existing business, Holiday Lighting Installation can be financially rewarding.

If you follow our step by step approach, you will be successful. This is not a get rich quick business. It will take hard work, dedication, commitment and a financial investment to make your venture successful.

 I wish you success in your new business venture.

Dennis Harvey

Chapter One: Advantages of Using Energy Efficient Holiday Lighting

Current Lighting Systems:

C-9 Incandescent

Mini Lights Incandescent

Traditionally, holiday lighting has used the mini-lights and C-7 / C9 incandescent lights as a standard (shown above). There are many disadvantages to using this 20th century light for holiday lighting. Some of these are:

* They use 90% more power than L.E.D. lights.

* They are very expensive without corresponding durability.

* Very brittle (made of glass).

* The technology is over 100 years old.

* Built in obsolescence. These last approximately three holiday seasons before going to the landfill.

* Only three strings can be connected together before a split has to be implemented.

* As color is painted on, it is subject to peeling.

* Due to high energy use, too many bulbs will trip a GFI and circuit breakers. This limits the number of strings that can be installed at one plug.

* They produce 90% heat and 10% light.

* All incandescent lights will be phased out by 2025.

Professional installation manuals suggest replacing 1/3 of incandescent bulbs every

year. This alone would add considerable material and labor to each job.

When installing incandescent lighting, it is necessary to calculate the amount of power consumed so there won't be any power failure due to circuit overload. If these calculations are not made correctly, just turning on a blow dryer can pop the GFI, resulting in a unhappy customer and an expensive service call for you.

As there is a limitation of three strings before splitting, inefficiencies such as extra time, material and labor to complete a professional installation are built-in.

GET THE PICTURE? DOESN'T THIS SEEM LIKE A HASSLE?

There is a better way than incandescent lighting. The answer is Light Emitting Diode Technolology (L.E.D.). The first L.E.D. Christmas light was put on the market for the 2002 season. The company we use has several international patents on the product. They are the pioneers and provide a superior product. This is the light we have used since 2003 with great success. More on this later.

Ten years ago, there wasn't a word about L.E.D. Today, the technology is rapidly evolving to outdoor accent lighting, flashlights, boat trailer and automobile lights. Why? Part of the reason is durability. Ask yourself if you have ever had a L.E.D. light go out on your computer, printer, cell phone, telephone? They last longer than the equipment they support.

This is not just a fad. It is the driving force replacing incandescent Christmas light bulbs.

Five years ago, one of our suppliers' catalogs had two pages on L.E.D. lights. In 2013, this same supplier devoted 35% of their catalog of L.E.D. lighting. That's quite a change in five short years.

In December of 2007, Congress passed an Energy Bill. Part of that bill included phasing out incandescent lighting. These lights began this phase out in 2012. All incandescent lights will be eliminated by 2025.

The manufacturers are gearing up for this. Bethlehem, GE, and most the major manufacturers are now offering L.E.D. Christmas lights. The quality and length of service vary among companies, but will range from 10,000 hrs to 200,000 hrs. In addition, the warranties vary from one year to limited lifetime warranties.

About L.E.D.

L.E.D. Lights have an estimated useful life of 50,00 to 200,000 hours of light, depending on the manufacturer. That can amount to up to 22 years of service.

 * Up to 25 strings (1500 lights) can be connected, without splitting, using residential grade lights. WIth commercial grade lights, over 3000 lights can be used without splitting, all on one 20 amp circuit. That's over six tenths of a mile!

* L.E.D. Lights generate no heat.

* The lights are epoxy injected molded with a solid seal. This makes them very difficult to break.

* They are non-fade, with scratch proof coloring. The color is in the molding and not painted on. This gives brilliant, consistent color.

* A big time saver: if one bulb fails, the remaining lights work.

* There is a failure rate of less than 1%.

* Outdoor/indoor rated flameproof and UL approved.

* With micro-chip technology, there are no filaments to burn out.

* L.E.D. lights put a major relief on the landfill.

* Operate at 10% energy cost of incandescent bulbs.

* Direct energy payback in 5-7 years.

* Patented faceting in the bulbs gives the illusion of twinkling when driving or walking past the display.

These lights are easy to work with, and customers love the brilliant colors and the fact that the energy savings is substantial.

The cost to run 12 strings (840 lights) of L.E.D. lights for 150 hrs during the holiday season at 12 Cents per Kilowatt is $69.12. Cost for 12 strings (1200 lights) mini-lite incandescent lights would be $604.00!

As an installer you will be way ahead of the competition in terms of cost of product, and have a great sales advantage with the energy efficiency of the L.E.D. lighting.

All of the graphics in this book are various types of L.E.D. lights and displays.

WHY PURCHASE THIS BOOK?

If this business seems appealing to you, there are several options you have to startup this business.

1. Start from scratch like we did. Go through the learning curve. This could be

very costly.

2. Purchase an expensive franchise for up to $15,000 and get lots of promises. Be restricted to a specific territory, and have to purchase all materials and equipment from them. Most of the franchises to date do not promote L.E.D. Technology.

3. Several manuals are available over the internet. These cost from $100.00 to $895.00, and most do not promote L.E.D. Technology.

4. We do not sell the lights or equipment. We rent the equipment to our clientele every year. This gives the customer the option to change colors and design annually. Additionally, this builds up equipment inventory and <u>makes our business much more profitable than if we sold equipment</u>.

5. Make an investment of the cost of this book and purchase our turnkey system for success.

The choice is yours! Buy this manual today and start making money using our methods that have been proven over the last 10 years.

Chapter Two: Starting Your Business 101

This chapter will discuss the basics of starting your business. If you have an existing business and are adding holiday lighting, you probably have done most what we will be discussing.

As there is a proliferation of information including many books on basic business start-up concepts. Therefore, we are not going to go into any great detail on these but will provide the important basics to get the ball rolling.

Define Your Goals

Get crystal clear on what you want this project or business to look like. Picture the details in your mind. Get a grasp of it and note how it feels from your perspective. When this is clear, write it down, addressing the following points:

- The primary purpose of your company and benchmarks for success. These will guide your direction for the business. Make sure you understand who you are serving and how you are serving them. This could be called your Strategic Objective or Mission Statement. An example is the following: "At Lights R Us, we bring light to our client's lives through the design and installation of LED holiday lighting. We strive to keep an affordable and beautiful solution for both commercial and residential customers while saving energy and our environment."
- Your business principles: Have your values written down. This is the Ten Commandments for your business. Here are some examples:
  - *We honor our word, we do what we say.*
  - *We avoid multitasking, we keep our focus.*
  - *We are the best and we do what it takes to be the best.*
  - *Read more here: http://www.holiday-lights.net/our-principles.html*

Working on getting a detailed vision can take some time. Let this process overlay your next steps below. We've found that it helps to have one sheet for your purpose, and a separate sheet for your principles. As they get exposed, write them down. As you finalize everything below, return to this and get it dialed in. Every project that we undertake I use the above technique to hash out the project before I invest a large amount effort in that project.

Choose Your Name

Naming a business is very important and should be one of the first steps in starting your business. It will be the foundation for the marketing, and sales material for your business. Try to get a name that does not limit you geographically. This will give you room for expansion. Using your own name is not a good idea for reasons that include a transfer of the business if it is sold after years of (hopefully) profitable operation. While considering the name, make sure to check with the State to see if that name is registered, then check with a domain name site such as GoDaddy.com to make certain you can use it.

Business Entity

This is the third major step you should make in starting your business. It is important that you have a legal designation for your business. It is not our intent to provide you legal advice; however we wish to provide some insight as to what is available.

There are 5 basic entities. Proprietorship, Partnership, Corporations and Limited Liability Companies, Non Profit Corporations.

Proprietorship: Easiest to form, however there is some liability and financial exposure to all of your assets, including your house, investment accounts and the business itself. This is the least expensive to establish, but in many cases the least desirable.

Partnerships: This entity has the same financial exposure as a proprietorship. These agreements need to be prepared by an attorney and are very specific.

Corporations: The most common corporate designations are C-Corporation and S-Corporations. The former is the type that most large businesses operate use. There are tax advantages with the C-Corp; however there are more operational requirements. The latter designation, the S-Corporation, is structured for smaller businesses. Liabilities in this designation are limited to company assets only, not your personal assets.

L.L.C. (Limited Liability Company) This is a blend of a Proprietorship, Partnership and Corporation. It has become more popular in recent years for small businesses. The paperwork is minimal, it is easy to form and limits owner liability. For tax purposes, it is filed with your personal tax returns and is easy to prepare.

We strongly suggest that you consult with an attorney and CPA before starting your business. They will be able to assess your personal needs and help you determine the type business entity that is most advantageous for you.

In Chapter 4, we budgeted $750 for forming your company. Attorney's charge up to $250.00 per hr. for their time. To keep expenses to a minimum you might have a 1/2 hr. meeting with an attorney to establish what is best for you. Call your local county bar association. They have a lawyer's referral service and they refer you to three attorneys who practice business law and will provide a 1/2 hr. initial consultation for about $30.00-$50.00. During the meeting, ask what additional startup costs might be so you can budget for the startup.

There are many companies over the internet who can do the paperwork for you. Be careful as it is important you get the job done right the first time. If you go this route, have an attorney review your documents before you take the next step.

Get Your Name and Logo Established

Designing a catchy logo is an excellent way to make you stand out. One of the best ways to get amazing graphic done is with 99 Designs: http://99designs.com/ . You will need business cards, stationary, envelopes and direct mailing cards. Also this entire design will go on your website, and installation trailer. Chapter 7 of this manual gives you more information on who to contact.

Register Your Business

Each State requires that you register your business. This information is available over the internet, usually under your State Corporation Division.

If you are a Corporation or L.L.C. Apply for your Employers Identification Number (E.I.N.). That can be Googled and done over the Internet. Go to www.irs.gov/business and it will walk you through the steps. There are internet companies that do the above for a fee. No cost directly with the IRS.

Business License

Most cities require that you have a business license. You can check with your local city to determine if this is the case for you. If so, the forms are generally simple and relatively inexpensive.

Bank Account

This should be set up as soon as possible to keep account of your expenses etc. Use a Bank that does not charge for commercial checking accounts. Apply for a company Visa. It will keep track of your spending on your business.

This about wraps up the basics to start your business entity.

Chapter Three: Estimating Your Startup Costs

The following is an estimate of startup costs for your L.E.D. holiday light installation business.

Many of the items you may have and it will not be necessary to purchase. This is especially true if you currently own or operate a business will a similar tool set. For example, Brennan owns and operates Solar Light, a premier Solatube dealership in Bend, Oregon. He had the tools, potential customers, time and manpower because of a slower Solatube season that he used to foray into his initial holiday lights season. We have listed below all the necessary items, and the spreadsheet can be modified with your own figures to arrive at estimated startup costs for your own business.

Our estimates are only a guideline for startup costs. For instance, the material costs below are an approximate value for the materials based upon an installation of 20 houses for the first year. You may adjust the figures accordingly if you wish to do more or fewer installations.

Everything else is a one-time investment, with the exception of the marketing, taking into consideration normal wear and tear and loss on equipment and materials. Extra spaces are left on the bottom of the spreadsheet for your customization.

We will go into detail on each of these items in Chapter 8, showing you direct suppliers, where to buy, when to buy and how to buy along with a detailed marketing timetable in Chapter 11.

The costs will vary depending on the area of the country you are in. Perhaps you have some of the equipment or can purchase pre-owned items, keeping your startup costs to a minimum.

L.E.D Holiday Light Startup Spreadsheet

Item:			Cost:	Totals:
Legal Incorporation			$750	$750
Office:				$900
		Computer & Printer	$600	
		Bookkeeping	$300	

		software		
		Building Website	$400	
		Website serving fees	$120	
Tools & Equipment				$3,980
		Trailer with Logo	$3,500	
		24' Extension Ladder	$200	
		8' Step Ladder	$85	
		8' Orchard Ladder	$85	
		10' Extension Wands	$20	
		Staplers	$40	
		Misc Tools	$50	
Marketing				$420
		Internet Marketing, including Google, Google Maps, Google adwords, etc.	$400	
		E-mail Blast	$20	
		Shared Revenue Marketing (groupon, living social, etc.)	$0	
		Cold calls to Commercial Property Managers	Sweat and time	
Materials	Inventory		Cost	Extended

	20	Timers	$20	$400
	1	500 ft Jump cord (build your own extension cord)	$200	$200
	120	male and female plugs for Jump and C-9 spool	.$25	$30
	10	3 way splitter	$1	$10
	1000 ft	C-9 Spool @ 12" spacing	$.25 a ft	$250
	1000	C-9 screw in LED bulbs	$1.05	$1,050
	20	25 ft mini and c-6 lights	$12	$240
	1000	3 way isolation clips for C-9 bulbs	$40 / case	$40
<Enter your own content here>				

Chapter Four: Five Year Business Projection

The following is a five-year projection based on starting with 20 installations, assuming an average job of $500 in the first year and 10 additional installations each year for the next four years. This is entirely achievable.

The key to success is customer retention. Repeat customers should be at least 50% of your business. This will reduce advertising costs to a point where the business can work on an all referral basis with little or no advertising. *With quality workmanship and good fundamental business skills, this is achievable within 3-5 seasons.*

Please note that the gross operating profit is before cost of labor and advertising which will depend on your local costs. We feel the figures below are on the conservative side, based on an average sale of $500 per installation and increasing by ten customers per year for four years, for a total of 60 customers by the fifth season. It is possible under ideal circumstances to do much more. For instance, Brennan's non-holiday light business had over a thousand customers. When he determined he wanted to start a "holiday lighting division" of his company, he sold fifty jobs his first year via a simple email blast to his existing customers.

Note that there are about 19 working days in November, not counting Saturdays, Sundays and Thanksgiving. As most clients wish to have their holiday lighting installed before or immediately following Thanksgiving, there are about five working days in December. This gives a total of 24 working days for installations, assuming a November 1 start. We've found that a two man crew can do approximately 72 jobs during the season. If sales were robust and it made sense to expand, another two-man crew could be added. Further, some of our friends that have holiday light businesses are starting work in early-to-mid October to take advantage of the longer daylight hours. This has multiple benefits, particularly in terms of labor efficiency and cash flow. We know of one business that starts earlier than the competition that is grossing over $100,000 a year in holiday light installations.

As a rule of thumb, a two-man crew can do an average of three installations per day, or roughly 2,000 feet of lighting installation. Based on our first-year sales projections (20 installations) and this rate of installation, first year installations would take approximately 6 working days to complete. Removing them is much quicker; it generally takes only about a third of the time to remove the lights as it does to install them. So, the total labor for a first year holiday lights startup would be about eight working days. At a cost of $14.00 per hr. per person, a two man crew would bring labor costs to $240 per day, or $4,480 for a full work season under this scenario. Obviously this is just one example. Owners can do the math based upon their goals, costs and ability to manage the business. Of course, if the owner does the work with one hired person, their overhead costs are greatly reduced - but then the Owner is working *in* the business instead of *on* the business, which can be problematic. In fact, it generally is. But that's another book.

As a rule of thumb, it takes about five years to build a new business to good financial footing and profitability. Below is a potential plan that makes sense to us:

Year	# Jobs	Material Cost	Sales	Gross Operating Profit
1	20	$3,535.00	$10,000.00	$6,465.00
2	30	$1,767.00	$15,000.00	$13,233.00
3	40	$1,767.00	$20,000.00	$18,233.00
4	50	$1,767.00	$25,000.00	$23,233.00
5	60	$1,767.00	$30,000.00	$28,233.00
6	60	$ 000.00	$30,000.00	$30,000.00

NOTE: Again, these projections are based on adding 10 customers per year starting the second year at an average of $500.00 per customer for 5 years. It also assumes a 100% retention rate. This is not realistic, but those clients that drop off can be replaced with new ones. It's just far more efficient to retain as many as possible, of course.

Year-1 Net Operating Loss

Year-2 Almost or Break Even

Year-3 Moderate Profits

Year-4 Good Profits

Year-5 Expand the business or maintain it at its present level. By then the business will have consistent cash flow and an established customer base. Not to be underestimated is the fact that this is a very enjoyable industry. There's something deeply satisfying about bringing holiday cheer to a family that is excited enough about the season to pay their hard-earned money for custom lighting. We sometimes find our employees singing Christmas carols while working on a customer's roof, to our customer's great amusement.

Now is the time to make the decision to go forward with the new business! It is infinitely customizable to your own life and lifestyle. You can take the costs and revenues and change to what goal you would want to have.

I strongly suggest starting slow the first year, getting a feel for the business, and establishing your four year growth plan.

The decision is yours. Good luck!

Chapter Five : Prospecting Your Potential Market

This is one of the easiest parts of starting your business. Best of all, it may cost absolutely nothing.

Statistically, the best return on an advertising investment is a professional company website and search-optimized Google. It is important that the website has the right keywords to drive customers to it (search optimization). Examples of good keywords for this purpose might include: "holiday lighting installation", "Christmas lighting installation", "install Christmas lights" and "L.E.D. light installation", to name a few. Google "Adwords" is a service provided by Google to help you in your search optimization efforts.

Another advertising method is Direct Mail. It is expensive contrasted to most types of advertising. However, if it's done correctly, a business can predict with some accuracy how many qualified leads will return per mailing. In addition, mailings can be adjusted to budgets and projected returns. Your mail piece should be of an effective size, full color both sides and direct. Show what your business can do, explain the benefits of L.E.D. holiday lighting, and motivate them to call you for an estimate or go to your website to obtain more information.

Email lists may also be purchased, and an "email blast" can be employed. This is nothing more than direct mail delivered electronically but can have tremendous results if properly executed. However, a business has to be very careful not to get labeled as a "spammer". It's best to consult with an expert on this marketing method before embarking upon it. As mentioned previously, Brennan employed an email blast and received 50 customers from it at the onset of his first year in the holiday lighting business. This was largely due to the fact that he had a good relationship with his existing customers and already stayed in contact via email, with their permission. But it can work even if this is not the case for a new business.

Whether employing direct marketing or an email blast, we advise targeting homeowners with an annual family income of over $100,000, and a home value that is in the neighborhood of $150,000 to $200,000 over the median price of homes in the target market area. This will vary throughout the country.

To determine the median price of homes in your market, contact a local realtor who has access to the Multiple Listing Service. These figures are readily available.

Once the median home price is determined, go to www.infousa.com Their website has a database that will provide the remainder of the necessary information. Once there, sort first by zip code, followed by the price of the targeted households. Try first with one zip code, as travel times - hence labor costs - can be more tightly controlled when operating within a single zip code.

After the target zip code is chosen, addresses within it can be purchased, downloaded and converted to labels for mailing. Email lists can also be purchased. As a general rule, email and physical lists are good for several years. Remember: people move, houses stay.

EXAMPLE. We chose a zip code in Bend, Oregon 97701. We know through Multiple Listing Service that the median home value is $250,000. We searched homes with a value of $450,000 to $1,000.000+ and found that there were 1,962 homes in that category.

A search by household income can also be conducted. For instance, try searching a $150,00 annual household income on the www.infousa.com site. Or a dual search of income and home value can be used to further define an ideal mailing list. These tools are important for determining the potential clients that comprise a target market.

We tracked our marketing for five years and found that direct mail gave us a consistent 6-7% reply. The national average for any type of mailing is about 1/2 of 1%. We assume that the reason for our increased success is that we targeted a specific market, with which we have experience. Importantly, when we reach out to potential clients we keep focused on who would be most likely to be able to afford our services.

With this response rate, a 1,000 piece mailer would generate between 60-70 responses. Our sales conversion rate from one of these inquiries runs about 50%. So, if we have 60 leads and convert 50% to customers, that gives 30 new customers. Thirty customers at a conservative average sale of $300.00 would generate $9,000 in revenue the first year. Keep in mind the above figures will vary on a sales team's ability to convert leads and inquiries to customers. Even with conversion or campaign response rates substantially lower than those we have experienced, direct mail and email blasts can be effective tools, especially at the onset of a new business or division of an existing business.

The great things about operating a business on one's own is that the sky's the limit. And what we've shared is by no means the full marketing story. We've said nothing about other potentially effective marketing concepts such as a professional, creative website, direct sales calls, logoed vehicles or trailers, coupon advertising, referrals generation campaigns, etc.

You may want to make an Excel spreadsheet on these figures and project and market accordingly.

No matter what marketing mix you use, it is all about TARGET MARKETING THE RIGHT PROSPECT. Experiment and have fun!

Chapter Six: Residential and Commercial Marketing

Effective Marketing is the key to success of any small business. We strongly suggest purchasing the book Guerilla Marketing by Conrad Levinson. www.gmarketing.com There are many different books in this series, most under $20. Pick the one that works for you.

In this chapter, we will provide some basic marketing ideas and some that are specific to the industry. There are a multitude of ideas that can be used, however it is very important to do the following:

1. Set up a system to TRACK THE SUCCESS of your marketing efforts. This can easily be done with an Excel spreadsheet, Google document, or a CRM such as Salesforce. Create "advertising sources" such as, Website Response, Google Ad, Logo Trailer, Media Response, Coupon Ad, Referral, Return Customer. Log each call and at the end of the season it will be apparent which tools are most effective. Contact Brennan at Brennan@holiday-lights.net if you would like a copy of his tracking system.

2. EXPERIMENT each year with different approaches. Don't let your marketing efforts go stale. There are multitudes of ways to market your services. Once you have your tracking system, emphasize the categories that work well. Use the following year to experiment with new ideas, while continuing to use the tools that worked the previous year.

3. See what your COMPETITORS ARE DOING. Talk with them, go to their website, check out their signs, etc. Always be aware of how your competitor is marketing their business. Are they using the same media outlets that your business uses? If so, how does their advertising come across? Analyze the pros and cons of their marketing as a potential consumer might see it.

4. NEVER stop marketing your business. Market, Market, Market.

Finally, we are going to review some of the marketing tools that we have used that have been successful. There are many others, however these are our favorites.

MAILING LIST: Regarding the mailing list, be sure to request that "Resident" or "Occupant" is written after the customer's name. This will prevent your the card from being sent back if the addressee has moved. People move, houses don't. This list is a one time (or at least infrequent) cost and can be used over and over. The list can be loaded into Excel. We suggest that a hard copy is printed and placed in a binder. Brennan makes two hardcopy lists; one by address and one by last name. He does this so he has a ready reference when calls come in, allowing him to check the success of his direct mail campaign. Also, it may be advisable to cover small areas by carrier route. Those labels can be printed out as well.

MAILING CARD: Your mailing card should be larger than a regular postcard so as to be less apt to be thrown away. It should be printed on both sides and should be in full color. The most economical printers are usually found over the Internet. We used www.vistaprint.com They provide reasonable service and it is possible to tie in business cards, envelopes and stationary all in one package. The cards can be created in a program called Printmaster. Be sure to change the final proof to a PDF File. Printmaster can do this. You might download from the internet a PDF conversion file which can convert *any* file to PDF. Please note that once you change a file to PDF it cannot be edited unless you have the full version of Adobe Acrobat, which may be a little spendy for your startup. To download, go to www.cutepdf.com. It will load as a printer option. Once it does, instead of choosing a printer use "cutepdf" and it will form the PDF file for you.

GRAPHICS: For us, www.99design.com is the most economical system to use, but you may have your own favorite. Whatever graphic you choose, save the file in PDF. This will be needed in order to send to Vistaprint. You can do your own or hire a professional to do it for you. Perhaps you have a friend or someone in the family who is good at graphics and can help you. Brennan has a design company that can also help. Because of his expertise in holiday lighting and marketing this could be a good place to get assistance. He can be reached at www.jediworks.com

DIRECT MAIL COMPANIES: Dennis used a mailing company the first year and found it very expensive for a small mailing. For 2000-2500 mail pieces, it is easier to just stamp and put labels on yourself. This can be done any time before the season. Note that the USPS has minimums for bulk mail.

COUPONS: Newspaper coupons can be a great source of leads. They come out weekly in most newspapers and a wide distribution can be achieved for costs in the $450 range. They often involve a discount or some other incentive for maximum effectiveness. Best results are achieved if they are bunched together with other coupons, in a coupon-book publication, for instance. Using them alone is not as effective. The downside is that because the leads are not qualified, coupons can result in a lot of tire kickers which can make employees less effective during the work day.

FLYERS: These may be produced in Word or Publisher and are great to leave with customers who are presented estimates. They can also be inserted in advertising mailers, Chamber of Commerce mailings or with a Service Club's monthly bulletin.

PRESS RELEASES: This technique works very well and is free. To write a press release, go to Google and download a free template that takes you all through the steps. Get local media emails or fax numbers and get the word out!

To get media addresses, it can be effective to search the Yellow Pages, although most are going from phone and fax to email. It may be time consuming to get all the addresses, however it will be a permanent part of your marketing plan. Sending faxes may be more effective than email. Many emails are deleted.

TELEPHONE BOOK:When you get your telephone number for your business it is suggested to forego purchasing Yellow Page advertising. We've found it to be very expensive and inefficient for this industry. We do recommend a listing in the Yellow Pages under "Holiday Decorations". Do not list a physical address, but it is important to lst the company web page address. In our experience, this costs about $12 per month. Calls begin to register starting as early as June or July.

TRAILER AND/OR VEHICLE LOGO (VEHICLE WRAP): This is your moving billboard during installations. Put your logo, telephone number and internet address on three sides in very large letters. Costs to have this done run about $500. The first two jobs you get from this advertising will pay for the graphics.

WEBSITE: A website is an important marketing tool to round out your full circle marketing plan. Unless you are good at web design, we suggest hiring a professional. If a professional designer is used, be sure your software will be compatible with theirs so you can go in and make occasional copy and graphics changes.

The website should be an informational. It should explain your services, educate the customer on L.E.D. lighting and motivate them to call you for an estimate. You will be surprised how many people go to your web site and email a request to be contacted. The consumer is constantly changing the way they do business.

One website that might be worth a visit is www.holiday-lights.net. It will give you ideas on how to form your own website.

As you can see, once the logo and basic copy for the business are designed, each of these marketing tools will tie into each other. Website, Google Ads, telephone, direct mail, vehicle wraps, flyers and coupons. You will have to experiment in your own market to see what works for you. Most of all, remember to *Never Stop Marketing Your Business!*

Chapter Seven: Working With Suppliers

In this chapter we are going to talk about the various suppliers we use to provide L.E.D. holiday lighting supplies. We will go category by category.

Diogen Foreverbrite L.E.D. Lights: These are the only lights that we use. They were the first to introduce the product and have worldwide patents on their systems. They fully warranty their products. Their website is www.holidaycreations.com. We use two suppliers for these lights. They are Kellogg Plastics in Smelterville, Idaho and Holiday LiteSource in Lubbock, Texas. There are other suppliers located in other parts of the country. These are listed on the Diogen website. Note that the lights are packed 12 per case. Freight costs are about $1.00 per string.

Kellogg Plastics: Call them 1-800-321-254, ask for Doris Miller and get on their email list. They will provide their current pricing for the year. This information usually comes out in the Spring. They carry a full line of Diogen Foreverbrite products. In addition, they manufacture various clips for attaching lighting to homes. They have the clips in bulk or retail packaging, but it's more efficient to buy bulk. They only stock L.E.D. lights, no incandescent. Order the lights in contractor's pack or bulk. The retail box packaging is time consuming to open a lot of cardboard goes to the recycler. They accept Visa and Mastercard. Ordering is by phone. They have bulk discount. We've found their service to be excellent.

Holiday LiteSource: They have a larger variety of L.E..D. lights and equipment for all types supplies for installing holiday lighting displays. Contact them by phone (1.800-762-2855) to get their annual catalog. It is mailed sometime around June/July. Product can be ordered by fax at 1-888-762-2852, email at orders@litesource.com or on their website at www.litesource.com. When you go to the website, you will have to register that your business sells "wholesale only" and not to the general public. You will have to provide a SSN if you're a proprietorship or an EIN if you are a corporation to purchase from them. They accept Visa, MasterCard, Discover and American Express.

Other Products ordered From Holidaylightsource are:

- All-In-One-Clip Product # 39301 or # 39301-Q.
- Oregon Fir Wreaths Product # WREATH-36-U-Or.That is an unlit 36" wreath. We use 1 string of L.E.D. lights per wreath.
- Oregon Fir Garland Product # Gar-914-u-or. 14'x9" unlit Garland. You need two to do a door and it takes 2 strings of L.E.D. Lights.
- Red Velvet Bows Product # Bow-16. 11"X116" bow. This goes great with the 36" Wreaths.
- Reach-N-Wrap Pole Attachment. Item # 35150. This can be

attached on the end of a painter's extension pole. A must if you are going to decorate trees. Buy at least 4 as they are brittle and break easily.

The above suppliers provide excellent service and offer volume discounts. Make sure to add about 8% to cover freight costs.

We use the C-6 & 24 ft. strings of L.E.D. lights in red, blue, green, multicolor, candlelight and pure white for our residential and small commercial customers. Multicolor is the choice of over 50% of our customers. Prices vary on colors, with white being the most expensive.

For larger commercial customers, we suggest commercial grade lighting. Commercial lighting has a different system of interlocking waterproof connectors that allow longer runs of lights without splitting. Up to 125 strings of lights can be run. That's 1500 C-7 or C-9 lights on 12" centers or 3,125 running ft. That's over ½ mile of holiday lighting on one 20 amp circuit. Try that with incandescent! (Actually, don't.)

The following suggested materials can be purchased from Wal-Mart, Home Depot, Lowe's or similar retailers:

- 24' Extension Ladder
- 8' Step Ladder
- 40' green extension cords
- 9' brown or green extension cords
- 3 way connectors and miscellaneous tools such as a hammer, diagonal pliers, extension wand, tool pouch, gloves etc.
- 8' Orchard Ladder. These are great for decorating trees. With a wand, heights of up to 25' can be reached comfortably and safely. If not at one of the stores above, they may be purchased at landscape supply distributors. One national company is Horizon. Go to the internet and see if they have a store near you.
- Timer. The only one we use is the Intermatic Raintight Outdoor Timer (model # HB31R). Most timers are 8 amp and this is rated at 15 amps. I have used over 65 of these timers without one failure. They're simply bulletproof. They should be ordered well ahead of season's start. They may give you a discount on 20. During the holiday season we usually run out of these.
- Stapler. We have gone through eight styles of staplers and the only one that works well is the Bostitch heavy duty cable tacker. We use both ⅜ and 9/16 cable staples. The longer staples are for permanent installs.
- Cargo Trailer. We use a 10' cargo trailer with opening doors on the rear and a side door. It will hold lots of stuff. You can build shelves. Order from local trailer dealer or buy used and have it wrapped or painted. You might consider ordering in red and installing a ladder rack. When you get it on the street, be prepared to get your customer's attention.

Chapter Eight: Hiring and Training Your Installers

Installers are a very important part of your company. If you have an existing business and you follow the installation guidelines below, the transition should be relatively easy.

Finding Employees: We have used Temp Agencies with good success. Their rates include worker's compensation insurance and they take care of all payrolls, etc. We suggest hiring two people that can climb ladders and want to work. We offer cash bonuses if they are conscientious and do a good job. The old cash carrot works almost every time. Note that it is easy work to train someone who has worked in the construction trades.

Other ideas would be to check with companies who have seasonal slowdowns and use one of their good employees.

How To Install LED Lights:

You will need some type of written installation procedure for your installers. We have the one we use which can be ordered over the internet in a Microsoft Word Template that you can change to suit your needs.

1. Determine the location of the outlet for the lights. It is preferable to locate it somewhere in the center of the installation. Keep in mind with L.E.D. lights you can continuously run up to 25 strings without splitting. The first step is to do is install the timer. We use portable drills and a 1 1/2 inch sheet rock screw and mount the timer. This makes a clean installation. The timer has an override that will keep it on. Turn it to "override" and install your lights turned on, or "live". There is a small chance that a bad string might be encountered. But it's usually the most difficult string at the peak of a roof that goes out. So don't take shortcuts.

2. Cords: If you are installing on trees, it works best to run your cords to the trees from the timer so everything will be installed live. Use a 3 way plug at the timer outlet when it is necessary to go different directions. If you are installing in front and back yards, it is better to run a long cord instead of using 2 timers. It is difficult to sync the timers and lights will not go on at the same time, making for dissatisfied customers and expensive callacks.

You will be using 2 types of cords. 40 ft. green 16/3 outdoor cords and 6-9 ft green or brown indoor rated cords. L.E.D. lights are not polarized so when using the short cords, the larger plug must be trimmed off if you are plugging into the L.E.D. light to attach more cords. Keep in mind that each string has two fuses. This is a safety feature should there be an exposed wire. The other tradeoff is to use 3 way plugs on the 40' green cords which will take more equipment. Do whichever you are comfortable with.

3. Attach your L.E.D. lights to the eaves, gutters etc., with the 3 way clips, using an interval of about 30 inches. If you are in an area with high winds or snow during the holidays, you should use about 24 Inch intervals. It is important to have the clips attached all the way onto the mounting surface. Wind and rain has a way of loosening strings. Make the wires as tight as possible. This will save yourself a service call. Another way of attaching strings is with a stapler. It is faster and is a much stronger installation. Use 9/16" staples. Be careful not to run a staple through the wire! This can also be bad news as lights go out and new fuses have to be installed. This is the other reason that lights should be installed live. It's best to have immediate feedback if a string is not going to work.

4. Trees. Sometime these can be difficult to install. Deciduous trees will take fewer strings than evergreen trees. With your 8" Orchard Ladder and a 10' wand, lights can be installed on trees up to 30'. We suggest installing a Reach-N-Wrap pole attachment on the end of your wand. Start at the top of the tree with the female end of the string. If you are on the ladder, you will need a helper to start winding the strings from the top to the bottom. You can help him with the wand by moving the ladder until you get the top 8'. When plugging your cord into the base of the tree, always leave your plug 12-18" above the ground. If it snows, you may not be able to unplug if there is ice, which increases uninstall time.

5. Garlands and wreaths make an attractive addition to any L.E.D. holiday light installation. Garlands may be attached to the entrance of the home. It generally takes two garlands to do the job properly. In addition, they look great along porch fences and railings. Garlands are attached using (3) 1/2 inch sheetrock screws. One is mounted in the middle, and two on the top of the door molding, about 12 inches out from the door. Then attach each garland at the middle and drape over each side. By doing it this way, both garlands will hang evenly. Then install 2 strings of L.E.D. lights to the garlands. After lights are installed, fluff the garlands as much as possible. Customers love them! Wreaths can be hung outside with one string of L.E.D. lights outside windows. Use a wreath hanger available from Holiday Litesource. Always check with the customer before drilling any holes!

6. Safety is always important when installing Christmas lighting. The ground can be slippery and icy. Always conform to O.S.H.A. requirements when working on ladders.

When the installation is complete, check all strings for lighting, set your timer correctly and check with the customer to see if they are satisfied with your installation.

7. Remember to thank the customer for their business and ask for referrals! Handing out fliers in the neighborhood takes only a few minutes and can result in immediate sales, sometimes on the spot!

Chapter Nine: Estimating Jobs

We've tried all ways under the sun to estimate jobs. We've taken pictures, completed diagrams and sent them over the internet, done them over the phone, etc. The system that we have developed works, takes little time, and provides accurate results.

Buildings

When installing holiday lighting on a building, try to silhouette or outline the lines of the building. Gutter lines, garage doors, windows, front entrances, pillars, porch railings and gazebos are the most common areas to outline. L.E.D. lights do not light up the building like incandescent do. They provide a silhouette of the structure you are decorating.

Trees and Shrubs

It is best to limit the height of decorations on trees to about 25 feet. With your orchard ladder and wand you can safely reach this height. If you go higher it will require equipment that is expensive to use.

Deciduous trees will take about 25% more lights than evergreen trees due to the fact that you can see through the branches. It just takes more lighting to make them look complete.

Shrubs and ornamental plants can be decorated with various colors and in different patterns to obtain very unique, pleasing results.

Trees use more lights than you would expect. A three foot tree will take one string, a four foot tree will take two strings and a six foot tree will take 3-4 strings. Always figure plenty of strings for trees. Customers will complain if there are not enough lights.

Interviewing the Customer

First and foremost: Be an expert! Make sure you have done your research, and can picture different holiday lights displays in your mind. One way to do this is to Google an image search for holiday or christmas lights.

When you first meet the customer, they may have a definite ideas about how they want their home or business decorated. I always ask them what they had in mind for their home. This gets a good positive dialog going and makes them feel more at ease. If they haven't a clue what they want to do, you can lead them along about the gutter line, roofline etc. to get a feel for their needs. Establish a tentative plan for their home.

You will next want to get into colors. Have a short cut sample string of C-9 lights with all colors on it. You can also have some mini lights, or C-6 lights. Try to light them in a dark place, such as their garage as the lights to not look appealing in a lighted area. Explain to them about the lights. They are sealed, so no moisture can enter, create no heat, and the color is not painted on but is in the epoxy and very difficult to break. And don't forget to mention the energy savings over incandescent lights. You want to establish a color plan. Multicolor on the roofing with red accents on the shrubs, a red roofline with green on the trees are a couple of examples. Do not use over 2 colors. This can look too busy and tacky.

We highly suggest filtering your customers. Do not take every job. Some customers are not fully clear in what they want, and this can haunt you. Try to filters these customers out. During your process of the sales interview, and definitely by the end of the estimate process, show the customer what you want it to look like with example photos. Either have a photo book of your work or another's work. Another method can include using a mobile device show the customer your website with examples, or even a Pinterest board of great examples. Ultimately, by the end of the estimate you and your customer need to be 100% on the same page with same vision of what it will look like.

Garlands and Wreaths

Add ons are great. A green garland with red lights makes a great statement on the entrance. Or wreaths in front of the windows with red and green lights. There are no wrong colors. Everyone has their favorites and I tell them all the colors of the lights look good in any combination. It's just a matter of personal preference. Brenna personally uses green and red on the garlands and wreaths at his home.

Pricing

Now that you have established an installation plan it is time to price the job. When customers ask what an installation costs either over the phone or at the job site, I often reply that our turnkey holiday lighting runs between $2 to $3 per running foot, depending on accessibility to the home. This includes design, materials, installation, maintenance and post-holiday removal. Don't throw some figure based on the size of their house and what kind of car they drive. Establish a structured pricing to justify the work that you will do. This is both more accurate and more ethical.

At that point it is a good idea to review with the customer what they would like and tell them you will measure their home and provide them a written proposal. The size of the job as well as how close we are to the holiday season often determines if we will be emailing the bid or estimating and doing the job immediately.

From here, let's show "Lights R Us's" exact procedure for estimating a job. A great thing to note is their use of current mobile technology. Lights R Us uses a program called evernote (evernote.com) to document and present a design layout.

The Lights R Us Procedure for estimate

Overview/ Purpose:

This procedure will document the process to estimate a job. In residential jobs we attempt to immediately go to install. It is important to note that we are very busy during the holiday lights season and if a customer wants only an estimate and there's a possibility we will not have time in the season actually do their job later.

Steps:

Prep:

1. If you're running early or late make sure that you have called the customer explaining your accurate timeline. It's best to simply be prompt.
2. Be neat and orderly, and in holiday lights uniform. The purpose of this is to convey confidence in your expertise. Be confident you are the expert, that you are the best.
3. Have your clipboard in order including:
    1. A fresh work order.
    2. A scratch sheet.
    3. A sufficiently charged mobile device.
4. Make sure your breath smells good, like a winter wonderland, or one of Santa's elves. Maybe the winter wonderland.

New Residential estimate:

1. When arriving, try to stay parked on the road if it all possible. Park in the driveway only as necessary.
2. Approach the home with your assistant if you have one. If your team is bigger than two people including yourself, leave the rest of the team at the vehicle.
3. Knock on the door and introduce yourself. A sample script might be aas follows: "Hello, I am (your name) and this is (helpers name). We are with Lights R Us and are looking forward to brightening your holiday season!" At the end of this pass a business card over to the customer.
4. Ask the customer if you can walk-through and see if she had any ideas of what she was looking for this year. It might help to walk around the property or area of install and dream with the customer. There will be times that the customer is going to look for your input so give advice and remember that you are the expert. Customers will generally be looking for suggested colors, etc. Dream big, and be creative!
5. When you have finished talking about all the ideas the customer has, explain to the customer that it will take you around X number of

minutes to get measurements and write everything up.

6. Take out your mobile device and use the **Evernote snapshot** to take pictures of all the areas that are going to be lit up. Remember to  be concise. Try to get angles that are easy to explain and incorporate the most amount of the lighting display. Do, however, take as many photos as necessary. After you are finished, save the photos and give a quick check to make sure that they are usable.

7. After clicking the check mark in Evernote and saving the pictures, systematically begin marking up the photos with the location of the lighting. We will use Evernote skitch to do this (http://evernote.com/skitch/). Also make sure the title of the Evernote is the name of the customer. (This should have auto filled from the calendar)

       1. Click on the image in the open Evernote;

       2. Click edit;

       3. If prompted complete action with skitch;

       4. Remember to use color coding for different sections of the bed so you can explain each aspect to the customer with the work order;

       5. Suggestion: use the straight line tool when marking up Eveline's as appropriate;

       6. Make sure you add text explaining which direction the pictures facing, effectively naming the picture.
          Example: North face, or South backyard.

       7. See this example:

Ranch house East

8. Note that in some cases photos will not be possible due to angle or other obstructions. In these scenarios we will need to draw up the lighting layout on our scratch sheet. This process often takes longer and should be only used as a backup.
    1. Use a ruler to make straight lines of the EE's;
    2. Note the trees;
    3. Bust out your art classes skills as needed for accuracy!
9. Above all, make sure that your documentation would be understandable if someone else was going to do this install. Make all your markups with this as the premise.
10. Once all the photos have been marked up, it is time to take measurements.
11. In the work order, write down the names of the subsections of the install. For example, you might say second-story eaves, first story eaves, west side windows, northside trees. Remember: designate North, South, East and West whenever necessary.
12. Measure:
    1. **Eave lines:** using the rolling measuring stick
        1. for straight sections walk with the measuring stick the linear distance of the

eve.

2. for pitched areas: measure from the lowest point of the triangle to the middle of the triangle. Estimate the pitch of the roof (4/12 (1.3), 6/12(1.4), 12/12 (2,). multiply your measured distance by the multiple associated with the pitch of the roof. Your equation should look something like this 12*1.3= 16 (round two of the next larger whole number)
3. Remember: this is only for half of the pitch so you will need to double this.
4. If you really want to get nerdy: we can use the Pythagorean theorem for this: $a^2 + b^2 = c^2$.
   1. A = the distance between the outer point of the eve in the middle of the triangle (in the example the numbers five);
   2. B = rise over run: estimate the pitch of the roof as above. 4/12 represents 4 inches of rise for every ft over. thus, A*4= B (would be 20 in the example);
   3. Square these numbers, add them together, and with the new number square root it;
   4. Thank you Michael Masterson for teaching me this at least 30 times, and I'm still not sure I get it hence the shortcut above.

2. **Banisters/poles:**
   1. With the tape measure measure the total distance around the banister: measure all sides, round up;
   2. measure the vertical distance of the banister. Call this "vert";
   3. Estimate the distance between wraps. This is often anywhere between 3 inches and 6 inches. Call this "spacing";
   4. Vert divided by spacing = wraps
   5. Adjust the wrap number to a whole and even number. Note that this will change the spacing!
   6. Multiply wrap * round = total distance of bannister;

7. Over time you will be able to eyeball this estimate pretty close and reverse this mathematics to get the spacing.

3. **Evergreen trees:**

1. With the rolling measuring stick measure around the outside of the bottom of the tree: in pict A) divide by half: Call this "round";
2. Measure or estimate the vertical distance of the Tree . Call this "vert";
3. Estimate the distance between wraps. This is often anywhere between 12 in to 32 inches. Call this "spacing";
4. Vert divided by spacing = wraps;
5. Adjust the wrap number to a whole and even number. Note that this will change the spacing;
6. Multiply wrap * round = total for tree in ft.
7. Over time you will be able to eyeball this estimate, pretty close and reverse this mathematics to get the spacing.

4. **Skeleton wrapped/deciduous trees:**

1. There is no mathematical way to estimate a skeleton wrap. You have to guess based on previous experience.
2. Now that all measurements are done, add them up in the sections that you had named earlier on the work order.
3. Use the example photo to guide the price for each section
4. On eave lines, when using C-9 Bulbs, duplicate the item with an isolation click bid which is at $3 per foot. This is chance to upsell the customer to a higher-quality install.
5. Once all the numbers have been filled out, return to find the customer.
6. Go over the Evernote markups with the customer to confirm that is everything you guys talked about. if you have missed anything go back to step seven.
7. Go over the cost with the customer. Work with them if they have a budget and tried it add and remove things as necessary to meet their need. Remember you do not want to waste your time doing all this estimate and not do the job.
8. Have the customer sign the work order and begin work, or schedule the work to be done later.
   1. Due to weather and the intensity of the holiday season we found that we will often not be able to get back to a customer. So we have made a suggestion to make sure they have a timeslot to go with at the time of the estimate.
9. **Remember at the end of the install to fill out the bottom of the work order, and add it to the customers' Evernote by opening the Evernote, editing it and adding a picture of the work order in paper scan mode. This updated work order should record the actual strings used, and how the customer paid.**

Commercial estimate:

1. Much like a residential estimate, a commercial estimate takes into the accounting of everything using Evernote and the work order the same.
2. For large commercial jobs exceeding $1000, these notes get converted onto a sheet explaining the job using this template: https://docs.google.com/a/solatubebend.com/document/d/1SrNAOek a53NpS9IpPWRxKAHemk0N9gU5BWlk_53kgNs/edit
3. The purpose is to explain more clearly each section of the commercial job, allowing the manager to add and remove things by individual building or section.
4. Further, we calculate the overall power savings, and financial savings so that the customer can see how much money they save and their environmental impact.

The Holiday Light Experts
541.306.4141
www.Holiday-Lights.net

WORKORDER

Customer Name: _____ Date: _____

Address: _____

$2 ft over 6 ft: Mini, Medium, and C-9
$4 ft over 6ft: Icicle Lights
$3 ft Premium Isolation Clipping

$3.50 ft: Icicle Lights
$1.50 ft under 6ft: Mini, Medium, and C-9

36" Wreaths: $60   20" Wreaths: $35
9 ft Garland: $35

Act. Strings	Item/Description:	Cost	Total Ft	Total Cost

Customer Signature:_____I have reviewed design with Lights R Us and read Policies. I agree.

HOLIDAY LIGHT INSTALLATION SERVICE POLICIES
2015

Thank you for Leasing our LED Holiday Lights. Due to increased vandalism by **Chipmunks (yes Alvin, Simon, and Theodore)** and to keep the costs down for our customers, we have the below policies. It is our intent to provide the best service that we can. However we will not be responsible for the following:

1. Vandalism or theft of lights or equipment.

2. Breakage of light strings, cords, or equipment due to severe wind, rain, snow, wildlife or other conditions beyond our control.

3. Light failure due to circuit breaker failure, or overload of circuits with additional customer added lighting.

Should the above occur, the customer will be responsible for replacements costs of the materials and time to repair the damage. We will invoice at our costs for the materials, a trip charge of $25.00 plus $36.00 per man hour in increments of 15 minutes.

We suggest that you be home at the time of the installation to be sure our crews will place the lights in the areas that we have agreed to. Should you wish to make changes or upgrades, our installers can provide you the cost at that time. Also if there some discrepancy, then they can resolve it at the time of installation.

If additional visits for installation are necessary, the above labor charges will be applied. There will be no charge if light strings fail for reasons not above.

We will make every effort to respond to service requests as soon as possible, and will provide you with the approximate date and time. However there may be unforeseen delays due to weather.

Brentata Ranch

Holiday Lights are a great way to communicate light and happiness in the dark winter seasons of Central Oregon. There is nothing like the glimmering of Christmas lights off the fresh still snow. This is why we at Lights R Us got into Holiday Lighting: to add to the natural beauty of Central Oregon with energy efficient holiday lighting.

Who is Lights R Us:

Lights R Us is a division of Solar Light. We are a family owned and operated business, licensed and bonded with the CCB *(#169755)*. We have been designing and installing Holiday Lighting arrays for the last 7 years for some of Central Oregon's most prominent buildings, and are **Certified Installation Consultants**. We love helping to communicate the joy of the holiday season by bringing light in the dark season.

We use LED holiday lights. Why? LED holiday lights use 10% the power of traditional lights, and last 10 times longer. This is how we got into the holiday lighting business; a passion for bringing light to peoples lives, merged with the opportunity to help be more harmonious with our natural world. A fun fact: if America moved all holiday lights to LED holiday lights, there would be a savings of 555,000 KWH a holiday season. WOW.

What we Do: Put up, maintenance, warranty, take down all lights, and store for the next season. Further we Maintain all lights for the season, and guarantee repair of any issues in a very timely manner.

The Break Down:

The Breakdown is broken into sections on each building so sections can be added or removed as necessary to achieve a matching a budget.

The Ranch House:
The Ranch House is the centerpiece to the Bratata ranch. Our suggestion is to wrap all eaves on the building with our warm white C-9 Bulbs. From the West we are suggesting to line up all

three levels of the building helping to promote the depths and size of the Ranch House.
In the Description Below Green and white colors represent feasible. Red color represent areas that will take special staging for proper safety equipment and booms.

1. East:
   a. Lower Eves (white): 180ft = $360
   b. Uper Eves (Red): 260 ft = $520
2. South:
   a. Lower Eves: (White): 70ft =$140
   b. Upper Eves: (Red): 64ft=$128
3. West:
   a. ~~Lower Eves (Green): 150ft =$300~~
   b. Mid Eves (white): 130ft =$260
   c. Upper Eves (Red): 162ft = $324
4. North:
   a. Lower Eves (White): 90ft = $180
   b. Upper Eves (Red): 64Ft = $128
5. Staging (See Staging Bid)
   a. Boom Truck
   b. Top safety rope harness installed
6. Total for all areas: $2040

Ranch house East

Ranch House South

Ranch house west

Ranch house north

Range:

The range building is open and inviting with its long linear view. Especially interesting is the Western exposure of curving lines setting a beautiful optical illusion that holiday lights would exemplify.

1. East:
   a. lower eves (white): 300ft: $600
   b. Gazebo walkway (white):122ft: $244
2. North:
   a. lower Eves white: 100ft: $200
3. West:
   a. Lower eves (white): 140ft: $280
   b. Gazebo eves (green): 42ft: $84
4. South: (nothing) :
5. ~~All upper eves (red): 260ft: $520~~
6. Staging (see staging bid):
   a. Boom lift:
   b. rope safety hook:
7. Total All: $1408

Gazebo:

The gazebo is in the parking lot of the range. it helps to give elevation transition between the range and the upper parking lot while also giving a beautiful accent to the long linear flow of the range. We are suggesting fully outlining the gazebo with the warm white C-9 lights that we have planned for the whole facility.

1. ~~All Sides: 120ft: $240~~	Gazebo

Barn:
The barn located at the north edge of the complex invites visitors as they drive up from the Trestle. It's magnificently steep slope really grabs the attention of someone as they come up. Our plan would be to wrap all Eveline's with our warm white C-9 bulbs. Due to the extreme pitch

of this roof, along with its metal roofing and no roof side safety hooks, a good portion of this building takes extra staging. Note there is a small section of the north roof that will not be accessed.

1. South
   a. Lower eves (white): 165ft: $330
2. West:
   a. ~~Eves (red):80ft: $160~~
   b. ~~window: 20ft: $40~~
   c. Carry lower eve square: 40ft=$80
3. North:
   a. lower eve (white): 165ft: $330
4. East:
   a. Lower eves (white) 25ft: $50
   b. Upper eves (red): 120ft: $240
5. Staging(see staging):
   a. Boom Lift
6. Total All: $1030

Barn east

Trestle:

The Trestle is the grand entry to the BratataRanch. We aim to line the area over the road on both East and West sides with warm white C-9 bulbs. These will give a magnificent combination with the existing trestle lighting to give a "Grand Entry" feel.

1. West: 75 ft: $150
2. East:75ft: $150
3. Total: $300

Trestle

Athletic Center:

To integrate the athletic center into the Grand complex we aim to have a simple and grabbing display over the entry.

1. ~~Upper eves (white): 90ft:$180~~
2. ~~Beams wrapped (Green): 148ft: $296~~
3. ~~Totals: $476~~

Athletic center north

Real Estate Office:

Again, we aim to keep it simple here trimming the eves with our warm white C-9, giving a framing of lights for the grand complex.

1. ~~West facing eves (White): 120ft: $240~~

Real Estate Office

Christmas Tree:

The Christmas Tree is what it is all about! We plan to wrap with warm white C-9 bulbs, with an estimated 8" of spacing between each horizontal wrap. We can reduce the density to match budget as necessary. The sample photo is at roughly 16" spacing.

1. Full wrap of 20ft tree:
   a. First 10ft at $1.50ft: 375ft: $562.50
   b. top 10ft at $2.00: 180ft: $360
2. Total: $922.50

Staging:

Due to the extreme pitch and height of the red marked areas our staging costs are a little high due to the need to rent a boom lift for one week of installation and one week of takedown. There are number of ways to reduce this cost:

1. If Bratata Ranch has a boom lift that we could use during the installation and takedown.

2. Solar light will install 2 roof safety hooks for $75

1. ~~60ft Boom Lift:~~
    a. ~~2 weeks rental: $1750~~
    b. ~~2 transport:$500~~
2. ~~2 roof saftey hooks: $120~~
3. ~~Totals Staging: $2370~~

Totals:

Our totals represent doing all aspects of each section. The first year we will see a discount of 15%, and in year 2 a discount of 22%.

1. **The Ranch House: $2040**
2. **The Range: $1408**
3. **The Gazebo: $0**
4. **The Barn: $1030**
5. **The Trestle: $300**
6. **The Athletic Center: $0**
7. **The Real Estate Office: $0**
8. **The Christmas Tree: $922.50**
9. **15% Discount: -$855**
10. **Staging: $75**
11. **Grand Total All: $4920**

Timing/Job site Prep:

We have set aside the week of Monday the 18th to work on this array. To complete our job safely it will be good for us to have an understanding of any events that will be going on during this week to coordinate which buildings we will work on.

The removal of the lights can be scheduled for any time that works for Bratata. Traditionally we remove lights the first weeks of January. However, many of our larger commercial clients prefer to leave the lights up until as late as March to celebrate the season.

While Supplies Last:

During the season our stock diminishes quickly, therefore from the time of drafting an estimate to the time of approval we may have committed the lights elsewhere and are unable to acquire more. In this case we will draft a supplement plan of equal value, and always sticking to our bid.

Energy Savings:

By Using LED technology for their holiday lighting, This Project will use an estimated **364** KWH (.14WPF). In contrast traditional holiday lights would use an estimated **12,992** KWH (5WPF). This is based on running the lighting arrays for 16 hrs, from Nov 20 to Jan 15 (56 day). Total estimated saving is **12628 KWH, equaling $1010.24 for the season.**
Total estimated environmental savings. 12628 KWH is equal to **63,140 pounds of CO_2** or equal to 63 Old growth Ponderosa trees.

Closing

Thank you for taking the time to consider making the switch to energy efficient LED holiday lighting with professional installation, maintenance, and storage for the next year. And it gets even easier after this. Next year all we have to do is call you in October to give you first pick at an installation date and the rest we already know. A few examples of our work for other business districts for multiple years now are; N.W. Crossing business district, Ameritel Inn & Suites (now The Hilton Garden Inn), 900 Wall Street Restaurant, The Inn at the Seventh Mountain, and the SunRiver SHARC facility.

Brennan & Melody Morrow
Owners
Lights R Us, Solar Light
541.306.4141
melody@solatubebend.com
www.holiday-lights.net
www.solatubebend.com

Chapter Ten: HOW TO GET REFERRALS AND REPEAT BUSINESS

To build your business you need referrals and repeat customers that use your services year after year. Remember, they have their lawns mowed, gutters cleaned, and irrigation services, so why not have your annual holiday L.E.D. light installation service?

The following is a list of ways to get referrals and repeat business:

1. Keep an accurate mailing list of all people to whom you have given estimates; even if they do not buy. Send them a reminder letter or email each year about your services. As we've said before, people move and houses don't. If it is upper-end home, maybe the next owner might like your services. Send them a postcard. You have the card and mailing label. All you have to do is add a stamp.

2. Provide your existing customers more than you said you would. This is called <u>added value</u>. Here are some ideas:

- Give them a Holiday Gift Certificate for one of the local businesses in the value of $10-15. Movie tickets are great.
- Add a wreath to their display at no extra cost.
- Buy some special Christmas ornaments for their tree at wholesale and give them one.
- Offer them a $25 discount for referring a friend or neighbor, or for early orders.

These are just a few suggestions. There are many ways to add value to a client. Be creative!

3. Right after Christmas, send your existing customers a thank you letter reminding them that you appreciate their business. Also tell them you will be picking up the lights the first 2 weeks of January and will send them a reminder letter in October of the following year. Also remind them, that if they want the lights off before you remove them, that they can simply pull the plug on the timer. This saves you a trip.

4. Make notes of businesses and homes that have their property professionally decorated. Jot the address down and send them a card the next season. Explain the benefits of using L.E.D. Lights.

5. Follow our "Timeline for Success" as explained in Chapter 11.

Chapter Eleven: Putting it all Together, a Timeline for Success

You have read the preceding chapters. Now is the time to put it all together. Following is an approximate chronological timeline to follow:

1. Develop a name and logo for the business.

2. Set up the corporate entity type. (L.L.C. Sub S. Etc).

3. Get all software, office equipment, stationery.

4. Develop the website.

5. Develop a residential marketing plan. Determine the number of direct mail pieces you will be mailing.

6. Develop a budget for marketing..

7. Design and order direct mailing pieces.

8. Develop press releases.

By September 15th:

1. Order L.E.D. lights, wreaths and garlands.

2. Have your mailing pieces stamped, addressed and ready to mail.

3. Purchase an installation trailer and have it wrapped.

Second Week in October:

1. Send out all direct mailing pieces.

2. Purchase cords, timers, ladders, and all installation equipment.

3. Implement marketing plan, including all marketing tools, coupons, press releases, flyers, etc. Contact commercial customers for installation. Start scheduling installations starting the first week of November.

First Week in November.

Start installations so you have time to complete all scheduled jobs on time. Remind customers that you are willing to do the install only, and then return to turn on the lights when they wish (generally the Friday after Thanksgiving).

End of the 1st Week in December.

All installations should be complete.

<u>Day After Christmas.</u>

Send a thank you letter to all your customers thanking them for their business and tell them you will be removing the lights starting the first day after New Year's. Remind them that they may turn off the lights by pulling the plug if they do not want the lights on after New Year's.

<u>Day after New Years.</u>

Start removing the lights.

<u>October 1st Following Year.</u>

Send out renewal letters to last year's customers and thank them for their past business.

Timing is important in this business. By following the above your installation season will run smoothly.

We wish you financial success in your new venture!

Dennis Harvey and Brennan Morrow

Disclaimer

The information contained in this book does not constitute legal advice. We have tried to provide accurate and reliable information however we do not make claims, promises or guarantees as to the accuracy or completeness of the information. All legal advice must be tailored to the specific person and their circumstances. In addition laws are constantly changing.

Nothing in this books should used as a substitute the advice of a competent Account and Attorney

The earnings or earning potential are examples only. You should seek competent financial advice from a C.P.A. or other qualified financial advisor before starting this venture. This is not a pie in the ski get rich quick business scheme and should not be entered into with that idea in mind.

www.ingramcontent.com/pod-product-compliance
Lightning Source LLC
Chambersburg PA
CBHW080649180526
45168CB00008B/3347